A Day in the Life of a SEA OTTER

A Day in the Life of a
SEA OTTER

Kay McDearmon
Illustrated with photographs

25

DODD, MEAD & COMPANY · NEW YORK

PICTURE CREDITS

Alaska Department of Fish and Game, Photograph by R. Wallen, 30
British Columbia Government, 43
California Department of Fish and Game, 10, 36 (Photograph by Ward Gillilan)
Karl W. Kenyon, 24, 38
James A. Mattison, Jr., 8, 11, 12, 15, 16, 18, 19, 21, 23, 26, 29, 31, 32, 35, 40, 45
John Mattison, 2
Picture Collection, California Academy of Sciences, 9, 37

To Jim

ACKNOWLEDGMENT

I am grateful to James A. Mattison, Jr., who has been researching and photographing California sea otters for fifteen years, for supplying his photographs and for reviewing my manuscript.

THE sea otter opened her
soft black eyes.
Once again she felt
the ocean waves rocking her.
She heard the roar of the surf,
and the loud bark
of the noisy sea lions.
A short distance away
she saw a flock of brown pelicans
gliding above the breakers.
She had slept on her back in a kelp bed,
less than a mile offshore,
with her pup on her chest.

At the first hint of darkness, she had scooped him up, and wrapped him in her paws.
Then she rolled herself and her pup over and over.
That way she wound them both in strands of giant kelp anchored to the ocean floor.

If she hadn't, ocean currents might have caused them to drift far away from the otter herd during the night. Or the powerful waves might have dashed them against the rocky California shore.

His father was living apart from them, with some other male otters of the herd.
A few days after his mother and father had met and mated,
she swam away while he was diving for food.
After her pup was born, she gave her baby all her love and attention.

Now, as the sea otter floated among the leafy kelp, she glanced at her baby.

He was still asleep. With her forepaws, she tenderly caressed his golden puppy fur.

Soon her pup awakened, and she helped untangle him from the the kelp,

and playfully ducked him a time or two.

Then, the fifty-pound mother felt hungry.

She was always a hearty eater. Today, if she were lucky,

she would stuff as much as twelve pounds of food into her glossy, round belly.

Now she swam on her back with her pup on her chest to her favorite feeding area.
To keep him safe, she hid him in a patch of brown kelp nearby.
Then she dived to the bottom of the sea.
She couldn't breathe underwater,
but she could hold her breath for as long as five minutes.
Yet she usually made a quick choice from among her favorite foods—
mussels, sea urchins, crabs, clams, squid, and abalone.
Now and then she dined on snails, starfish, or sea cucumbers.
Sometimes she surfaced with a single shellfish clutched in her forepaws.
Other times she hauled up an assortment of goodies,
perhaps as many as a dozen clams or snails and three or four sea urchins.
All these she tucked into the loose, pouchlike skin under her forelegs.

For her first course this morning, the sea otter captured a purple, spiny sea urchin.

She also brought a smooth stone to the surface.

She had plans for it,

as the sea otter is one of the few mammals, besides man, that uses tools regularly.

She lay on her back, and carefully placed the stone on her chest.

With both forepaws she held the urchin,

and pounded it against the stone until she smashed the shell.

Then she scraped out the soft insides with her teeth.

In the sea otter's next haul there was a mussel.

This time she had to work much harder to break the shell.

It took her thirty-five blows against the stone on her chest.

Meanwhile, a sea gull bobbed on a nearby wave, watching for a chance to grab some of the otter's breakfast. She splashed water on the gull's face with her webbed hind feet, and the annoyed bird flew away.

She had just broken open a clam and was about to eat it,

when another sea gull swooped down beside her.

He nipped her on the tail, and she dropped the clam.

The crafty gull picked up his prize and soared into the sky with it.

A few minutes later, the sea otter was enjoying a crab when a towering wave came along.

It swept away the last chunk of crabmeat from her dining table.

During her breakfast the sea otter didn't forget her pup.

Each time she surfaced she checked to be certain

that he was safe before she began eating.

Once he had drifted away from the kelp bed.

She swam over to him, and carefully deposited him back there once more.

This time she placed a strip of kelp across his chest.

The seaweed would keep him from floating away.

Many dives later the sea otter finished her meal.

She shoved the crumbs left on her chest into the sea.

She washed her forepaws and face.

She even washed behind her tiny ears, and brushed off her white whiskers.

Afterward, she groomed her thick, velvety brown fur.

The sea otter was careful to remove every crumb
and speck of dirt from her fur.
Anything that remained, even slime from fish,
or a film of oil from a passing ship could mat her coat.
Then the cold water and wind could reach her skin and chill her.
It might even kill her.
The sea otter seemed to know this,
for she cleaned her fur completely many times during the day.
That way her dense fur trapped a layer of air that kept her snugly warm,
much as blubber protects seals and whales.

Now it was time for her pup's breakfast.

She swam over to him, picked him up,

rolled him over on her furry stomach, and allowed him to nurse.

When he had swallowed all the warm milk he wanted,

she flipped him over, and gave him a soapless bath.

She licked his face and woolly fur with her pink tongue,
like a cat cleaning her kitten. Then with her teeth she dug into his deepest fur.
The pup squirmed, but his mother didn't lessen her efforts.
After the sea otter finished grooming her pup,
she rewarded him with a ride on her chest.

He put his paws over his eyes to shield them from the sun's bright rays.

As the sun warmed his body, he felt drowsy.

And with his mother crooning softly to him, he soon fell asleep.

She slipped away from him, leaving him floating upon the surface.

For a time she, too, floated on the ocean, like a giant dark brown cork.

Then she paddled along on her back, moving her hind flippers up and down.

Finally, she tired of this, and rolled over.

She could swim faster on her belly, but she seldom swam that way,

except when she was in a hurry, as in trying to escape an enemy.

Soon after her pup awakened,
the sea otter raised her head
higher out of the water,
and quickly looked around.
A shark, a killer whale,
or a fishing boat
could mean danger.
A slashing propeller blade
could cut her.
Or an angry abalone fisherman
might shoot at her.
But just now all was clear,
so she gave her pup
a swimming lesson.

Her pup had floated easily from the day he was born and opened his eyes.
When he was only a few weeks old,
she was teaching him to swim on his stomach.
Now she wanted her little one to swim on his back.
So she swam a little ahead of him, and waited for him to swim to her.
She kept coaxing him this way
until he was so tired he couldn't kick his flipperlike feet any longer.
Then she swam back to him. Cradling him in her forepaws, she kissed him.

The pup was also learning to dive, but pushing downward was hard for him.
Millions of tiny air pockets in his fur kept him afloat,
much as the air in a life preserver keeps a human being from sinking.
But the pup would have to learn to dive all the way to the bottom of the ocean,
as almost all the food he liked was there.
It would be weeks before he would have the strength and skill
to dive about seventy feet to the sea floor.
Then, for awhile he would help his mother gather food.
When she leaves him, sometime after his first year,
he will collect all his own food.

But today the sea otter was so pleased
with her pup's swimming
that she allowed him to swim
a little farther away than ever before.
A few older pups of the herd were playing
together, and he joined them.
Their watchful mothers, like his,
were close by.
This was a real treat for him.
He raced, played leapfrog, and
wrestled with the other pups.
Feeling in a mood for mischief,
he ventured over to the kelp
where some male sea otters were resting.
He spotted a sleeping, white-headed male
and pulled him under the water.

Sea otters are usually amiable animals. They rarely fight even when
another otter steals their food. But two males may occasionally fight at mating time.
This morning the old male that the pup ducked was angry at having his sleep disturbed.
So he chased the pup. The pup squealed loudly. Within seconds
his mother was racing to help him. She grabbed him by the shoulder
just as the old male was catching up with him.

Soon the sea otter was hungry again.

She swam with her little one to their earlier feeding areas.

During one dive she saw a red abalone clinging to the underwater rocks.

She grabbed a stone, and slammed it against the abalone's shell.

The abalone loosened his grip on the rock, and the sea otter quickly captured it.

This time the sea otter didn't catch enough food to satisfy her huge appetite.

So she traveled with her pup to still another feeding area.

When the pup saw his mother open a mussel, he rose out of the water, and whimpered.

She had fed him tidbits before, and knew that he really liked mussels.

So she swam over to the kelp bed to him, and held out the remainder in her paw.

He seized the morsel and ate it eagerly.

Afterward, mother and pup played together for a long while.

They turned somersaults, and ducked each other.

They tossed seaweed from paw to paw.

And once the pup dared to tweak his mother's whiskers.

She didn't mind at all.

Later that afternoon the little one
played with another pup who appeared nearby.

Meanwhile, his mother floated on her back
with her flippers out of the water,
and her forepaws folded across her chest.
A chocolate brown sea lion swam toward her.
She watched him approach,
ready to dive to safety if need be.
But the sea lion was looking for a friend.
As he glided alongside the sea otter,
he gently nuzzled her.
Soon the two of them were riding
up and down the wild waves together.
Now and then the otter,
swimming on her belly,
leaped out of the water and plunged
into the sea again,
as porpoises also love to do.

Once when she leaped, she saw a gray whale propelling his huge bulk
through the water, a sea gull resting upon his back.

The sea otter kept on frolicking. From her own mother she had learned
that gray whales do not attack otters. So she wasn't afraid of them.

Suddenly, she heard her pup's wail.
She couldn't see his head bobbing above the waves,
or tell his location from his frightened cry.

So she cried out, too, hoping that he could hear her.

Then, fearing that he was really lost, she began hunting for him.

She swam swiftly on her belly, going first one way, then another.

Finally, she found him behind a high rock.

She grabbed him, and cuddled him in her forepaws.

Once again mother and pup snacked, napped, and played together happily for hours.

Then from overhead a sea gull
squawked out an alarm.
This, the sea otter knew,
might mean that hungry killer whales
were headed their way.

She outwitted such whales before.

Once she escaped by diving deep and far.

Another time, aware that killer whales avoid getting tangled in kelp,

she raced to the kelp bed, and hid there until the danger was over.

Once when time was short, she lay still,

and the whale mistook her for a water-soaked log.

Once she doubled up and played dead.

Killer whales attack only living prey, so they passed her by.

But now she had a pup.

She would never desert him, but escaping with him would be a handicap.

He wasn't likely to lie quietly until the killer whales passed.

And he couldn't stay submerged as long as she could.

She seized the side of her pup's neck in her teeth, and dived.

When she surfaced, he squealed. As soon as he caught his breath,
she dived a second time. She dived with him again and again.

Each time she surfaced, her noisy pup cried.

But each dive brought her closer to the kelp bed.

Meanwhile, the few killer whales searching for food were getting closer.

The sea otter couldn't yet see their high black fins above the water.

But when she surfaced, she could hear the steady beat of their flukes.

She was tiring, but she dared not rest yet.

With all the strength she had left, she dived once more, and dashed for the kelp bed.

This time she made it.

Mother and pup were safe at last.

Later, she dived for her supper, fed her pup, and snacked on bits of seaweed.

As the sun slid into the west,

she swam back to the herd with her pup on her chest.

Then she wrapped herself and her pup in ribbons of kelp.

She felt the ocean waves gently rocking her.

She glanced at the moonlit sky.

She saw a cluster of stars, then only two, then one, and soon, none at all.

Her eyes were closing, and she and her pup were drifting off to sleep.

THE AUTHOR

Kay McDearmon was born in San Francisco and received her B.A. degree from the University of California at Berkeley. A former high school teacher and social service worker, she is the author of numerous newspaper and magazine articles. It was an article on sea otters that prompted her interest in introducing them to young children in this, her first book.

Kay McDearmon lives with her husband, a professor of Speech Pathology, in Turlock, California, where leisure time activities include golf, bicycling, swimming, reading, and music.